I0454459

Title: Transformative Path: Exploring Sanctification's Power

Outline:

Introduction

- Definition of sanctification

- Importance of spiritual growth

- Preview of the transformative journey

Chapter 1: Understanding Sanctification

- Explaining sanctification in religious and spiritual contexts

- Historical perspectives on sanctification

- Theoretical frameworks and perspectives

Chapter 2: The Power of Transformation

- The significance of personal transformation

- Exploring the impact of sanctification on individuals and communities

- Real-life examples and case studies

INTRODUCTION

In the tapestry of human existence, the quest for spiritual growth and personal transformation has remained an enduring pursuit. At the heart of this journey lies the profound concept of sanctification—a process that transcends religious confines to illuminate a path towards inner enlightenment and external grace.

Welcome to "Transformative Path: Exploring Sanctification's Power." Within these pages, we embark on an odyssey to unravel the mysteries of sanctification and harness its transformative potential in our lives. Whether you're seeking a deeper connection with the divine, a pathway to self-discovery, or a means to impact the world around you, this journey holds keys to unlock the doorways to personal and collective evolution.

Throughout history, sanctification has emerged as a beacon guiding seekers across cultures, faiths, and philosophies. Its essence lies not merely in rituals or dogmas but in the resonance it strikes within the human spirit—the call to transcendence, the beckoning towards a higher state of being.

In this exploration, we'll delve into the very fabric of sanctification: its definitions, historical significance, and its manifestations in the lives of individuals and communities. We'll unveil the power it wields to shape destinies, reshape mindsets, and stir the soul towards profound metamorphosis.

Yet, this journey is not a solitary pursuit. It's a shared odyssey—where wisdom, experiences, and insights merge to illuminate the path ahead. This eBook is not just a guide but a companion—a compass pointing towards the realms of growth and enlightenment.

As we navigate through the chapters that follow, prepare to delve into the depths of spiritual growth, overcome barriers, and embrace the transformative potential that lies within. Whether you are taking your initial steps or are already on this journey, "Transformative Path: Exploring Sanctification's Power" invites you to venture further, to seek deeper, and to discover the boundless possibilities of a sanctified existence.

Let us embark together on this transformative path—where the ordinary transcends into the extraordinary, and the mundane is touched by the divine.

Definition of Sanctification:

Understanding Sanctification: A Journey Towards Holiness

Sanctification, a term steeped in spiritual depth and significance, transcends the mundane to encapsulate the very essence of the human quest for divine alignment and moral purity. It stands as a beacon across myriad faiths and philosophical doctrines, resonating with the fundamental human yearning for spiritual growth and transformation.

At its core, sanctification embodies the process of becoming holy or sacred. It represents a journey—a deliberate, ongoing endeavor towards moral and spiritual perfection, marked by a dedication to align one's thoughts, actions, and essence with the divine or revered principles. This pursuit of holiness spans various religious traditions, each offering unique perspectives and practices while sharing a fundamental aim: the elevation of the human spirit towards higher realms of existence.

Within Christian theology, sanctification stands as a pivotal doctrine. It embodies the progressive, transformative work of the Holy Spirit within believers, guiding them towards greater conformity to the likeness of Christ. This process involves a lifelong journey of spiritual growth, marked by purification from sin, spiritual maturity, and a deepening relationship with God.

In Judaism, sanctification finds resonance in the concept of kedushah, signifying separation or consecration. It involves the designation of certain objects, spaces, or times as sacred and the call for adherents to live a sanctified life by adhering to moral and ritual purity laws.

Similarly, within Islam, the process of sanctification, referred to as tazkiyah, revolves around purifying the soul from vices and enhancing virtues. It involves a spiritual journey marked by self-discipline, seeking closeness to the Divine, and cultivating a heart free from spiritual ailments.

Beyond these Abrahamic traditions, sanctification resonates in diverse spiritual practices across cultures and faiths. Whether through meditation, prayer, rituals, or ethical conduct, the quest for sanctification remains a universal pursuit—a yearning to transcend the ordinary and embrace the sacred.

Sanctification isn't merely a theoretical construct; it's a lived experience—an intimate dance between the human and the divine. It encompasses not only personal transformation but also influences communal harmony and societal ethics. Its effects ripple through relationships, communities, and the broader fabric of humanity, fostering empathy, compassion, and a sense of interconnectedness.

This journey towards sanctification isn't without its challenges. It demands introspection, self-discipline, and a willingness to confront one's imperfections. It requires humility to acknowledge shortcomings and resilience to persevere through setbacks. Yet, it offers an unparalleled opportunity for growth, guiding individuals towards a life of purpose, meaning, and spiritual fulfillment.

In essence, sanctification embodies the noble pursuit of aligning oneself with the sacred, transcending limitations, and evolving towards a state of spiritual wholeness—a journey laden with significance, depth, and the promise of a transformed existence.

The Significance of Spiritual Growth: Nurturing the Soul's Evolution

Spiritual growth stands as an essential facet of human existence, encompassing the profound journey towards self-discovery, transcendence, and a deeper connection with the divine or the universe at large. In a world often consumed by material pursuits and external achievements, nurturing one's spiritual dimension holds immense significance—an importance that resonates across cultures, beliefs, and philosophies.

At its core, spiritual growth transcends the confines of religious dogma to encompass a universal pursuit—a quest for meaning, purpose, and inner peace. It invites individuals to delve into the depths of their being, unraveling layers of consciousness, beliefs, and values to uncover a profound truth—their essence beyond the physical realm.

One of the pivotal aspects underscoring the importance of spiritual growth lies in its capacity to provide a compass for navigating life's complexities. In moments of adversity, uncertainty, or existential questioning, a robust spiritual foundation serves as a guiding light—an anchor grounding individuals amidst the tempests of life. It offers solace, wisdom, and a broader perspective, enabling individuals to transcend transient challenges with resilience and equanimity.

Moreover, spiritual growth fosters emotional resilience and mental well-being. It provides a framework for introspection, self-awareness, and emotional regulation, equipping individuals with the tools to navigate their inner landscapes. Through practices like meditation, prayer, or mindfulness, individuals cultivate a heightened sense of awareness, leading to reduced stress, anxiety, and an enhanced ability to cope with life's upheavals.

The pursuit of spiritual growth isn't solely an inward journey; it extends its tendrils outward, influencing relationships, communities, and the world at large. As individuals undergo transformation and cultivate virtues such as compassion, empathy, and altruism, these qualities ripple through society, fostering harmonious interactions and collective well-being. Spiritual growth, therefore, becomes a catalyst for societal evolution—a cornerstone for building cohesive, compassionate communities.

Moreover, it provides a framework for moral and ethical conduct. By aligning actions with deeper spiritual values, individuals contribute to a more just, equitable, and compassionate world. It inspires a sense of responsibility towards oneself and others, fostering a collective consciousness rooted in principles of love, understanding, and tolerance.

In essence, spiritual growth isn't a luxury but a necessity—a vital aspect of holistic well-being. It transcends religious affiliations, cultural boundaries, and personal ideologies to nurture the very essence of humanity—the soul. It offers a pathway towards inner fulfillment, resilience, and a deeper understanding of the interconnectedness that binds all living beings.

As we embark on the journey of spiritual growth, we uncover layers of wisdom, cultivate virtues, and evolve towards a more profound sense of purpose—a journey laden with significance, transformative potential, and the promise of a more enlightened existence.

Preview of the Transformative Journey: Embarking on the Path of Evolution

Welcome to the threshold of a transformative odyssey—a journey that transcends the ordinary to unravel the profound mysteries of self-discovery, spiritual growth, and the pursuit of sanctification. This journey isn't a mere passage through time and space; it's an exploration of the depths of our existence—a quest that beckons us to venture beyond the familiar confines of our comfort zones.

The transformative journey is an invitation—an invitation to delve into the recesses of our being, to confront our truths, embrace our vulnerabilities, and dance with the essence of our authenticity. It begins with a whisper—an inner calling that tugs at the strings of our soul, urging us to embark on a path less traveled—a path laden with uncertainties, challenges, and boundless opportunities for evolution.

As we step onto this transformative path, we relinquish the confines of stagnation and embrace the fluidity of growth. It's a passage that demands courage—an audacious leap into the unknown, a willingness to shed the layers of societal conditioning, and a commitment to embrace the discomfort of self-exploration.

This journey isn't a solitary endeavor; it's a communal pilgrimage—a convergence of wisdom, experiences, and aspirations. Along this path, we encounter fellow travelers—kindred spirits whose stories resonate with ours, whose struggles mirror our own, and whose triumphs inspire our courage. Together, we form a tapestry—a tapestry woven with the threads of shared insights, collective wisdom, and the unwavering resolve to evolve.

The transformative journey unfolds across landscapes—landscapes of introspection, contemplation, and self-realization. It invites us to traverse the valleys of introspection, scaling the peaks of self-awareness, and navigating the twists and turns of spiritual awakening. It's an expedition marked by revelations—a tapestry woven with epiphanies that illuminate the path ahead, guiding us towards profound self-discovery.

Yet, this journey isn't without its tests. It's a labyrinth—riddled with doubts, fears, and moments of uncertainty. It challenges our convictions, tests our resilience, and beckons us to confront our shadows. But within these crucibles lie opportunities—opportunities to transcend limitations, to transcend limitations, and emerge reborn—a testament to the transformative power inherent within.

Ultimately, the transformative journey isn't just a passage from one point to another; it's a metamorphosis—a metamorphosis that transcends the self, enriches the soul, and unveils the boundless potential inherent within each of us. It's an initiation—an initiation into a world where the ordinary surrenders to the extraordinary, where the mundane is touched by the divine.

Chapter One: Understanding Sanctification

Exploring Sanctification in Religious and Spiritual Contexts

Sanctification, a concept deeply rooted in religious and spiritual doctrines, resonates across diverse traditions, embodying the pinnacle of spiritual evolution and moral purity. Within various religious frameworks, sanctification assumes multifaceted dimensions, each offering a unique lens through which individuals seek divine alignment and spiritual elevation.

Christian Perspective:

In Christian theology, sanctification holds a central position as a transformative process facilitated by the Holy Spirit within believers. It encompasses a threefold aspect: positional sanctification, where believers are declared holy upon acceptance of Christ; progressive sanctification, denoting the ongoing growth towards moral purity and Christ-likeness; and ultimate sanctification, the culmination of this process upon entry into the divine presence.

The Apostle Paul's writings emphasize sanctification as a lifelong journey—a process of renewal and transformation. It involves shedding the old self, embracing virtues, and conforming to the image of Christ. Through prayer, scripture, sacraments, and the guidance of the Holy Spirit,

Christians endeavor to live sanctified lives, embodying virtues such as love, humility, and compassion.

Jewish Perspective:

Within Judaism, sanctification manifests in the concept of kedushah—separation or consecration. It involves designating certain objects, spaces, or times as sacred and the call for adherents to live a sanctified life by adhering to moral and ritual purity laws outlined in the Torah. Sanctification in Judaism extends beyond individual transformation to encompass communal sanctity, with rituals and observances aimed at elevating everyday life to a sacred realm.

Islamic Perspective:

In Islam, the process of sanctification, termed tazkiyah, revolves around purifying the soul from vices and enhancing virtues. It involves a spiritual journey marked by self-discipline, seeking closeness to Allah, and cultivating a heart free from spiritual ailments. Through practices such as Salah (prayer), fasting, charity, and Dhikr (remembrance of Allah), Muslims strive for inner purification, aiming to attain a state of spiritual excellence and closeness to the divine.

Universal Spiritual Perspectives:

Beyond specific religious paradigms, sanctification resonates in universal spiritual practices. Various traditions emphasize the purification of the soul, seeking unity with the transcendent, and embodying virtues like compassion, humility, and altruism. Practices such as meditation, mindfulness, service to others, and self-reflection serve as pathways toward sanctification, facilitating spiritual growth and inner harmony.

Common Threads:

Across these diverse religious and spiritual contexts, sanctification converges on common themes—an aspiration for moral purity, alignment with divine principles, and the cultivation of virtues. It underscores the human quest for transcendence, inviting individuals to embark on a transformative journey towards a more enlightened existence.

In conclusion, sanctification stands as a cornerstone within religious and spiritual landscapes—a testament to the enduring human pursuit of spiritual growth, moral excellence, and a deeper connection with the divine.

Historical Perspective on Sanctification: Tracing the Evolution of a Spiritual Concept

The concept of sanctification, with its roots deeply embedded in human history, traces a nuanced journey across civilizations, theological doctrines, and philosophical discourses—a journey that unfolds the evolution of spiritual thought and the quest for moral elevation.

Ancient Origins:

Sanctification finds its early traces in ancient civilizations, where rituals, purification practices, and ceremonial acts sought to consecrate individuals, spaces, or objects as sacred or divine. In Mesopotamia, Egypt, and other ancient cultures, the separation of the sacred from the profane formed the basis of sanctification—a practice that established a connection between the mortal realm and the divine, fostering a sense of reverence and spiritual significance.

Hebrew Scriptures and Early Christian Thought:

Within the Hebrew Scriptures, sanctification emerges as a recurring theme. The notion of holiness permeates the text, emphasizing separation, purity, and consecration. The Israelites' covenant relationship with God mandated sanctification, delineating laws and rituals aimed at fostering a sacred existence.

In early Christian thought, the writings of the New Testament expounded upon sanctification, framing it as a transformative process facilitated by divine grace. The teachings of Jesus Christ and the apostles emphasized moral purity, spiritual growth, and the renewal of the inner self—the foundational aspects of the sanctification process.

Medieval and Renaissance Periods:

During the medieval period, Christian theologians such as Augustine and Thomas Aquinas contributed to the discourse on sanctification. Augustine highlighted the role of divine grace in the process of moral purification, emphasizing the necessity of God's intervention for human salvation. Aquinas further developed the concept, integrating Aristotelian philosophy with Christian theology, elucidating sanctification as a transformative journey towards union with God.

The Renaissance witnessed a revival of interest in individual spirituality and personal growth. Mystics like Meister Eckhart and Teresa of Ávila emphasized the inner journey towards spiritual perfection—a quest for sanctification through contemplation, self-reflection, and union with the divine.

Modern Interpretations:

The advent of the Protestant Reformation led to diverse perspectives on sanctification. Reformers like Martin Luther emphasized justification by faith but also highlighted the significance of sanctification as the ongoing process of moral transformation. John Wesley, the founder of Methodism, emphasized the pursuit of holiness as an essential aspect of Christian life, advocating for a practical theology that encompassed both justification and sanctification.

Contemporary Relevance:

In the contemporary era, sanctification continues to resonate across religious and spiritual traditions. Its historical evolution has paved the way for diverse interpretations, accommodating the spiritual aspirations and beliefs of individuals in an increasingly pluralistic world. Today, sanctification stands as a timeless concept—a testament to humanity's enduring pursuit of spiritual growth, moral purity, and a deeper connection with the sacred.

Theoretical Frameworks and Perspectives on Sanctification

Sanctification, as a multifaceted concept embodying spiritual evolution and moral purity, has been approached and interpreted through various theoretical frameworks and perspectives. These diverse lenses shed light on the intricacies of the sanctification process, offering insights into its mechanisms, implications, and significance within religious, philosophical, and psychological discourses.

Religious and Theological Perspectives:

Within religious traditions, sanctification often serves as a linchpin—a transformative process guided by divine intervention or spiritual practices. Theistic frameworks, whether in Christianity, Judaism, Islam, or other faiths, emphasize the role of the divine, grace, and adherence to religious precepts in the sanctification journey. The theological lenses underscore concepts of divine intervention, repentance, purification, and ethical conduct as pivotal elements shaping sanctification.

Psychological and Philosophical Frameworks:

Psychological perspectives offer a lens through which sanctification is viewed as an intrinsic part of human development and well-being. Psychologists such as Abraham Maslow and Carl Rogers explored the concept of self-actualization—a process akin to sanctification—where individuals strive for personal growth, self-realization, and the fulfillment of their potential.

Existentialist philosophers like Viktor Frankl highlighted the significance of finding meaning and purpose in life—an aspect resonating deeply with the quest for sanctification. They emphasized the individual's responsibility in creating their meaning and pursuing a higher purpose, paralleling the journey towards moral and spiritual elevation.

Developmental and Growth Perspectives:

Developmental psychologists and theorists, including Erik Erikson and Lawrence Kohlberg, proposed models of moral and psychosocial development that mirror aspects of the sanctification process. Their theories highlight stages of moral reasoning and identity formation— stages akin to the progression towards higher ethical standards and spiritual maturity inherent in the sanctification journey.

Interdisciplinary Approaches:

Contemporary scholarship often adopts interdisciplinary approaches to understand sanctification. Scholars integrate theological, psychological, sociological, and philosophical perspectives to unravel the complexities of spiritual growth and moral development. This convergence of disciplines offers a holistic understanding of sanctification, acknowledging its multifaceted nature and diverse implications across human experiences.

Contemporary Relevance and Challenges:

In the contemporary landscape, sanctification faces challenges within a rapidly changing societal context. Pluralism, secularization, and evolving belief systems pose questions about the universality and relevance of sanctification. Yet, these challenges also spark dialogues, fostering innovative interpretations and applications of sanctification within diverse contexts, adapting its principles to resonate with contemporary sensibilities.

In essence, the theoretical frameworks and perspectives surrounding sanctification offer a tapestry of insights—a convergence of religious, psychological, philosophical, and developmental understandings. This mosaic of perspectives enriches our comprehension of the sanctification journey, underscoring its timeless relevance in the quest for spiritual growth, moral refinement, and the pursuit of a more meaningful existence.

Chapter 2 The Power of Transformation

The Significance of Personal Transformation: A Journey Towards Wholeness

Personal transformation stands as a cornerstone of human existence—an odyssey that transcends the boundaries of the self, fostering growth, evolution, and a deeper understanding of one's being. It encapsulates the essence of change—a metamorphosis that extends beyond superficial alterations to encompass a profound reorientation of the mind, heart, and soul.

At its core, personal transformation represents a pilgrimage—an inward journey towards self-discovery, self-realization, and self-actualization. It beckons individuals to embark on a path less traveled—a path illuminated by self-awareness, introspection, and a willingness to confront the depths of one's being. This transformative odyssey unfolds through various facets, each bearing immense significance in shaping the course of an individual's life.

Unveiling Authenticity:

Personal transformation unravels the layers of conditioning, societal expectations, and inherited beliefs, unveiling the authentic self—the essence beyond masks and facades. It fosters a deeper understanding of one's values, passions, and aspirations, empowering individuals to live in alignment with their true essence. This quest for authenticity liberates the spirit, instilling a sense of purpose and fulfillment rooted in genuine self-expression.

Empowering Growth and Resilience:

Through personal transformation, individuals cultivate resilience—a resilient spirit capable of adapting to life's adversities and embracing change. It nurtures an adaptive mindset, enabling individuals to navigate challenges with fortitude, learn from setbacks, and emerge stronger. The process of transformation becomes a crucible—an arena where resilience is forged, enabling individuals to transcend limitations and discover untapped potentials.

Facilitating Healing and Empathy:

Transformation entails healing—a process that involves acknowledging wounds, addressing past traumas, and fostering emotional well-being. As individuals undergo personal transformation, they not only heal their own wounds but also cultivate empathy and compassion towards others' struggles. This journey of healing extends beyond the self, fostering connections and nurturing an empathetic understanding of shared human experiences.

Cultivating Purpose and Contribution:

Personal transformation fuels the quest for purpose—a search for meaning beyond the mundane. It inspires individuals to seek avenues where their unique gifts and talents converge with the needs of the world. This pursuit of purpose fosters a sense of contribution—a desire to make a meaningful impact, leaving a legacy that transcends individual existence.

Embracing Transcendence:

Ultimately, personal transformation culminates in transcendence—a state where the individual transcends egoic limitations, embracing interconnectedness with the universe or a higher power. It leads to a broader perspective, fostering a sense of unity, and guiding individuals towards a deeper understanding of the human experience.

In conclusion, personal transformation isn't merely a journey; it's a profound metamorphosis—a metamorphosis that transcends the individual, influencing relationships, communities, and the world at large. Its significance lies not only in the evolution of the self but in its ripple effect—a ripple that resonates with the transformative power inherent within each individual.

Exploring the Impact of Sanctification on Individuals and Communities

Sanctification, with its inherent power to elevate the human spirit and foster moral purity, resonates deeply within individuals and reverberates across communities, exerting a transformative influence that transcends the boundaries of the self.

Impact on Individuals:

1. Spiritual Growth and Moral Development:** Sanctification serves as a catalyst for individuals' spiritual growth, nurturing a deeper connection with the divine and facilitating moral development. It inspires a pursuit of higher ethical standards, guiding individuals towards virtues such as compassion, empathy, and integrity.

2. Enhanced Well-being and Resilience:** Embracing sanctification often leads to enhanced psychological well-being and resilience. Individuals undergoing sanctification develop a sense of inner peace, reduced stress, and an increased ability to navigate life's challenges with fortitude and equanimity.

3. Personal Transformation:** Sanctification fosters personal transformation—a journey of self-discovery and self-realization. It enables individuals to shed limiting beliefs, embrace authenticity, and live in alignment with their core values, leading to a more purposeful and fulfilled existence.

4. Increased Empathy and Altruism:** As individuals progress on their sanctification journey, they often cultivate empathy and altruism. This heightened sense of empathy allows for deeper connections with others, fostering a spirit of compassion and a desire to contribute positively to society.

Impact on Communities:

1. Cohesive and Compassionate Communities:** Sanctification's influence extends beyond the individual, shaping communities characterized by empathy, understanding, and cooperation. Communities centered around sanctified principles often exhibit greater social cohesion and a willingness to support and uplift one another.

2. Ethical and Moral Foundations:** Sanctification within communities establishes ethical and moral foundations, guiding collective decision-making processes and fostering a culture of integrity, fairness, and justice.

3. Social Responsibility and Service:** Communities driven by sanctified values often prioritize social responsibility and service to others. Acts of

charity, volunteering, and community outreach become integral components of communal life, nurturing a sense of shared purpose and communal well-being.

4. Conflict Resolution and Reconciliation:** Sanctification encourages communities to seek reconciliation and resolution in times of conflict. The emphasis on forgiveness, understanding, and empathy fosters an environment conducive to healing and reconciliation, promoting harmony and unity within the community.

Collective Transformation:

Ultimately, the impact of sanctification on individuals and communities transcends mere personal growth or communal harmony—it signifies a collective transformation. It nurtures a collective consciousness, wherein shared values, empathy, and a sense of interconnectedness create a tapestry of harmonious coexistence, contributing to a more enlightened and compassionate society.

In conclusion, sanctification's impact extends far beyond the individual's spiritual journey—it permeates the fabric of communities, instilling virtues, fostering connections, and paving the way for a more empathetic, ethical, and harmonious societal landscape.

Real-Life Examples and Case Studies: Sanctification in Action

Example 1: The Life of Mahatma Gandhi

Mahatma Gandhi, an iconic figure in India's history, exemplified sanctification through his principles of non-violence (Ahimsa) and spiritual resilience. His commitment to truth, simplicity, and service to others transformed not only his own life but also mobilized communities towards social change. Gandhi's pursuit of moral purity and his unwavering dedication to justice inspired a nation, leading to India's independence and influencing civil rights movements globally.

Example 2: Mother Teresa and the Missionaries of Charity

Mother Teresa, revered for her selfless service and compassion, embodied sanctification through her dedication to the poorest of the poor. Her unwavering commitment to serving the destitute, sick, and dying in Kolkata, India, transcended mere charitable acts—it reflected a sanctified life devoted to alleviating suffering and spreading love to those marginalized by society.

Case Study: Desmond Tutu and Reconciliation in South Africa

Archbishop Desmond Tutu played a pivotal role in post-apartheid South Africa, advocating for reconciliation and healing through the Truth and Reconciliation Commission (TRC). His emphasis on forgiveness, empathy, and truth-telling paved the way for a nation torn by racial divisions to embark on a journey towards healing and unity. The TRC process, guided by sanctified principles, aimed not only to address past injustices but also to foster reconciliation and national cohesion.

Contemporary Examples:

1. Civil Rights Movements: Leaders like Martin Luther King Jr., guided by sanctified principles of justice and equality, spearheaded civil rights movements that transformed societies and catalyzed legislative changes aimed at eradicating racial discrimination.

2. Global Humanitarian Efforts: Organizations like Doctors Without Borders, driven by sanctified values of compassion and service, provide medical assistance to vulnerable communities worldwide, transcending political boundaries to alleviate suffering.

3. Individual Transformation Stories: Numerous personal accounts showcase the transformative power of sanctification in overcoming personal struggles, addiction, trauma, and adversity, leading to renewed lives focused on positive contributions to society.

Chapter 3: Spiritual Growth and Development

Stages of Spiritual Growth: Navigating the Path to Enlightenment

Spiritual growth unfolds through a series of transformative stages, each marking a milestone on the profound journey towards self-discovery, higher consciousness, and a deeper connection with the divine or universal essence. These stages, often interwoven and non-linear, encompass the evolution of the human spirit, guiding individuals towards greater spiritual maturity and enlightenment.

Stage 1: Awakening or Initiation

The journey typically begins with an awakening—a moment of realization or initiation, where individuals experience a profound shift in consciousness. This awakening can be triggered by various factors such as a spiritual experience, a personal crisis, exposure to profound teachings, or an intense desire for inner fulfillment. It marks the beginning of the quest for deeper meaning and purpose in life, setting individuals on the path towards spiritual exploration.

Stage 2: Seeking and Exploration

In this stage, individuals engage in seeking and exploration—a period marked by curiosity, inquiry, and a thirst for spiritual knowledge. They explore diverse traditions, philosophies, and practices, seeking resonance with teachings that align with their inner truth. This phase involves learning, introspection, and contemplation, laying the foundation for a more profound understanding of self and the universe.

Stage 3: Purification and Self-Reflection

As the journey progresses, individuals enter a phase of purification and self-reflection. This stage involves inner work—addressing past wounds, releasing attachments, and purifying the mind and heart. Through practices like meditation, self-inquiry, and self-discipline, individuals confront their egoic tendencies, fostering inner peace, and emotional healing.

Stage 4: Expansion and Connection

The expansion and connection stage signify a deepening connection with the divine or universal consciousness. Individuals experience a sense of interconnectedness with all beings, transcending the boundaries of the self. This phase involves experiencing moments of transcendence, profound insights, and a heightened sense of unity and love, leading to a deeper understanding of the interconnectedness of all existence.

Stage 5: Service and Integration

At this stage, individuals feel called to serve and integrate their spiritual insights into everyday life. The focus shifts from personal growth to selfless service, compassion, and contributing positively to the world. They integrate spiritual principles into actions, relationships, and endeavors, embodying virtues such as compassion, altruism, and integrity.

Stage 6: Union or Oneness

The final stage culminates in union or oneness—a state where individuals experience a profound sense of unity with the divine, the universe, or the cosmic consciousness. This stage transcends intellectual understanding, leading to a direct experiential realization of one's divine nature. It represents the pinnacle of spiritual evolution—a state characterized by inner peace, unconditional love, and a profound sense of purpose.

Practical Steps Towards Sanctification:

Cultivating Holiness in Daily Life

Sanctification, while embodying a lofty spiritual ideal, unfolds through practical, actionable steps—daily practices and intentional actions that foster spiritual growth, moral refinement, and a deeper connection with the sacred. These steps, when integrated into daily life, serve as a roadmap towards cultivating holiness and aligning oneself with divine principles.

Step 1: Self-Reflection and Introspection

Begin the journey towards sanctification with self-reflection. Allocate time for introspection, examining thoughts, emotions, and actions. Journaling, meditation, or moments of solitude facilitate self-awareness, enabling individuals to identify areas for growth, acknowledge shortcomings, and set intentions for personal transformation.

Step 2: Cultivating Virtues and Ethical Conduct

Sanctification involves cultivating virtues aligned with spiritual principles. Practicing kindness, compassion, honesty, patience, and forgiveness in daily interactions fosters moral integrity. Strive to embody these virtues in both personal and communal interactions, anchoring actions in ethical conduct guided by sanctified values.

Step 3: Prayer, Meditation, and Mindfulness

Engage in practices that nurture spiritual connection. Regular prayer, meditation, or mindfulness sessions provide moments of communion with the divine. These practices cultivate inner peace, deepen spiritual awareness, and serve as anchors for aligning thoughts and actions with sanctified intentions.

Step 4: Study and Contemplation of Sacred Texts

Dive into the wisdom offered by sacred texts or spiritual teachings. Engaging in study and contemplation of these texts provides insights, guidance, and inspiration for sanctified living. Reflect on the teachings, applying their wisdom to daily life for personal growth and moral guidance.

Step 5: Acts of Service and Charity

Engage in acts of service and charity, extending kindness and support to others. Volunteering, helping those in need, and contributing to the well-being of the community foster a spirit of selflessness. Service-oriented actions align with sanctified principles, nurturing empathy, and fostering a sense of interconnectedness.

Step 6: Seek Community and Mentorship

Connect with like-minded individuals or seek mentorship from spiritual guides. Engaging with a supportive community or mentor offers guidance, encouragement, and accountability in the sanctification journey. Shared experiences and communal practices reinforce the pursuit

Tools for Spiritual Development:

Certainly! Sanctification, within the realm of spiritual development, refers to the process of becoming more like the divine or achieving holiness. It's a multifaceted journey that incorporates various tools and practices aimed at nurturing one's spiritual growth. Here are some fundamental tools and practices utilized for spiritual development via sanctification:

Prayer

Prayer stands as a cornerstone in the pursuit of sanctification. It's a direct channel for communication with the divine, fostering a deepening relationship and understanding of spiritual principles. Different traditions and faiths offer diverse forms of prayer, whether it's through meditation, recitation of sacred texts, or silent communion.

Meditation and Mindfulness

Engaging in meditation and mindfulness practices allows individuals to cultivate inner peace, focus, and spiritual awareness. By quieting the mind and observing thoughts without judgment, one can tap into a deeper understanding of self and existence.

Study of Sacred Texts

Exploring and studying sacred texts relevant to one's spiritual tradition provides guidance, wisdom, and insight. It involves delving into the teachings, principles, and stories contained within these texts to gain a deeper understanding of the divine and how to embody its virtues.

Spiritual Community and Fellowship

Being part of a spiritual community or fellowship offers support, guidance, and opportunities for shared learning and growth. Through congregational worship, discussions, and shared practices, individuals are nurtured and encouraged in their spiritual journey.

Acts of Service and Charity

Engaging in acts of service and charity aligns individuals with selflessness and compassion, nurturing a sense of connection with others and the divine. It's a practice that transcends personal desires and contributes to the betterment of society.

Self-reflection and Examination

Regularly reflecting on one's thoughts, actions, and intentions promotes self-awareness and accountability. This introspective practice helps individuals identify areas for growth and transformation.

Spiritual Retreats and Pilgrimages

Participating in retreats or embarking on pilgrimages provides opportunities for solitude, reflection, and connection with the divine in unique settings. These experiences often lead to profound spiritual insights and personal transformations.

Guidance and Mentorship

Seeking guidance from spiritual mentors or teachers who have traversed the path of sanctification can be invaluable. Their wisdom, experience, and guidance can help navigate challenges and provide clarity on the spiritual journey.

Rituals and Ceremonies

Rituals and ceremonies embedded within spiritual traditions serve as symbolic acts that deepen one's connection with the divine. They offer a structured framework for spiritual practice and growth.

The journey of spiritual development via sanctification is deeply personal and multifaceted. Integrating these tools and practices into daily life creates a nurturing environment for spiritual growth, enabling individuals to progress towards greater spiritual fulfillment and alignment with the divine.

Chapter 4: Overcoming Challenges

Obstacles on the Path of Sanctification:

Certainly! Obstacles on the path of sanctification can present themselves in various forms, hindering an individual's pursuit of spiritual growth and alignment with God's character. These hurdles can arise from internal struggles, external influences, or a combination of both.

One significant internal obstacle is the human condition itself. Our innate tendency towards sin and imperfection creates a constant challenge in the pursuit of sanctification. Despite our best intentions, we may find ourselves repeatedly falling into patterns of behavior or thought that contradict the ideals of sanctification. Overcoming these deeply ingrained habits and inclinations requires consistent effort, self-reflection, and reliance on divine guidance.

Another internal hurdle is the battle of the mind. Negative thoughts, doubts, and self-criticism can derail progress on the path of sanctification. An individual might struggle with feelings of unworthiness, inadequacy, or a sense of failure, impeding their spiritual growth. Overcoming these mental obstacles involves cultivating a positive mindset, nurturing self-compassion, and filling the mind with uplifting and affirming spiritual truths.

External influences also pose significant challenges to sanctification. The pressures of the world, societal norms, and cultural values often conflict with spiritual principles. These external factors can tempt individuals away from their pursuit of sanctification by promoting materialism, selfishness, and individualistic pursuits over selflessness and spiritual growth.

Moreover, relationships and social circles can either support or hinder one's journey of sanctification. Negative influences from peers or a lack of understanding and support from loved ones can create obstacles on the path to spiritual growth. Navigating these relationships while remaining committed to the pursuit of sanctification requires discernment, boundary setting, and sometimes making difficult choices about associations.

Furthermore, unforeseen life circumstances such as hardships, tragedies, or unexpected challenges can shake one's faith and pose significant obstacles on the path of sanctification. Coping with these difficulties while maintaining a strong spiritual foundation can be incredibly challenging.

Addressing these obstacles involves various strategies. Cultivating self-awareness, practicing self-discipline, and engaging in regular spiritual disciplines such as prayer, meditation, and scripture study can strengthen one's resolve and resilience. Seeking guidance and support from a spiritual mentor, counselor, or supportive community can provide invaluable assistance in navigating these hurdles.

Understanding that the journey of sanctification is not without challenges is crucial. Embracing these obstacles as opportunities for growth and drawing closer to God, rather than as insurmountable barriers, is a vital mindset in overcoming them. Ultimately, perseverance, faith, and reliance on God's grace are key in navigating and triumphing over the obstacles on the path of sanctification.

Strategies for Overcoming Spiritual Hurdles:

1. Embrace Spiritual Disciplines: Engaging in consistent spiritual disciplines is foundational. Regular prayer, meditation, scripture study, and participation in a faith community provide essential spiritual nourishment. These practices help align thoughts, actions, and desires with the principles of sanctification.

2. Cultivate Self-awareness: Developing a deep understanding of one's inner self, including strengths, weaknesses, and triggers, aids in overcoming spiritual hurdles. Recognizing patterns of behavior or thought that hinder sanctification enables intentional efforts to address and transform them.

3. Community and Mentorship: Surrounding oneself with a supportive community or seeking guidance from a spiritual mentor offers accountability, encouragement, and wisdom. Sharing experiences, struggles, and triumphs with others fosters growth and provides valuable perspectives.

4. Resilience and Perseverance: Embracing setbacks as opportunities for learning rather than as failures is key. Building resilience through perseverance helps overcome discouragement when facing spiritual hurdles, fostering a mindset of continuous growth.

5. Surrender and Trust: Learning to surrender control and trust in divine guidance is pivotal. Accepting that the process of sanctification is a partnership with God allows for humility and openness to guidance, enabling spiritual growth.

6. Intentional Mindset Shifts: Shifting one's mindset from a focus on perfection to progress is crucial. Acknowledging that sanctification is a journey allows for patience and self-compassion amidst challenges.

7. Guarding Influences: Being mindful of external influences and setting boundaries against negative influences aids in maintaining sanctification.

Choosing associations, entertainment, and activities that align with spiritual values strengthens commitment to the journey.

8. Gratitude and Celebration: Cultivating an attitude of gratitude and celebrating small victories fosters a positive outlook and motivation. Recognizing and acknowledging progress, no matter how small, encourages perseverance.

9. Forgiveness and Self-Compassion: Practicing forgiveness, both towards oneself and others, is liberating. Embracing self-compassion in moments of struggle or failure allows for grace and enables moving forward in the journey of sanctification.

10. Continuous Learning: Remaining open to learning and growth through ongoing education, spiritual exploration, and seeking deeper understanding of faith principles enriches the sanctification process.

Overcoming spiritual hurdles through sanctification is a dynamic and deeply personal journey. Employing these strategies, coupled with patience, faith, and reliance on divine guidance, empowers individuals to navigate challenges, grow spiritually, and move steadily forward in their pursuit of sanctification.

Addressing Doubts and Setbacks:

Addressing doubts and setbacks in the realm of sanctification, or the process of becoming more Christ-like, is a common experience for many individuals on their spiritual journey. Sanctification involves a transformation of the whole person—mind, body, and spirit—towards becoming more aligned with the character of God.

One of the primary challenges individuals face in this process is doubt. Doubt can arise from various sources: questioning one's progress, struggling with persistent weaknesses, or feeling disconnected from spiritual growth. These doubts can be unsettling, but they are a natural part of the human experience and the spiritual journey. Embracing doubt as an opportunity for growth rather than a setback is crucial.

Firstly, it's essential to recognize that doubts don't invalidate progress or commitment. Doubts often arise precisely because an individual is earnestly engaging with the process of sanctification. Embracing doubts can lead to deeper introspection, a renewed commitment to spiritual practices, and a more profound understanding of one's faith.

Secondly, setbacks are a normal part of any transformative process. In the context of sanctification, setbacks might include struggles with particular sins or habits that seem insurmountable. However, setbacks don't define the journey; they are moments to learn, grow, and deepen reliance on God's grace and guidance.

Addressing doubts and setbacks in sanctification involves several strategies. Seeking guidance and support from a spiritual mentor, counselor, or community can provide invaluable perspective and encouragement. Engaging in regular spiritual practices such as prayer, meditation, scripture study, and participation in a faith community can also offer strength and clarity during times of doubt.

Moreover, reflecting on past successes and growth can be a powerful reminder of God's faithfulness in the sanctification journey. Celebrating small victories and progress, even amidst doubts and setbacks, can provide motivation and inspiration to continue forward.

Remembering that sanctification is a lifelong process helps individuals approach doubts and setbacks with patience and grace. It's essential to be kind to oneself and recognize that growth often happens gradually, sometimes imperceptibly.

Chapter 5: Living a Sanctified Life

Integrating sanctification into our daily life

Integrating sanctification into our daily lives involves infusing spiritual principles, practices, and virtues into our routine activities, thoughts, and interactions. Here's an exploration of how this integration can manifest across various aspects of life:

Mindfulness in Daily Actions

Incorporating mindfulness into everyday tasks helps anchor us in the present moment. Whether it's mindful eating, walking, or working, paying attention to each action fosters a sense of awareness and connection. For instance, savoring each bite of a meal or being fully present during a conversation enhances the depth of experience and cultivates gratitude.

Ethical Decision-Making

Applying moral and ethical principles derived from one's spiritual beliefs guides decision-making processes. When faced with choices, considering how they align with spiritual values aids in making decisions that promote harmony, compassion, and justice.

Compassionate Communication

Integrating sanctification involves nurturing compassionate communication. Practicing empathy, active listening, and speaking with kindness and honesty fosters healthier relationships and promotes understanding and harmony within our interactions.

Service and Acts of Kindness

Regularly engaging in acts of service and kindness towards others embodies the essence of sanctification. Whether through volunteering, assisting someone in need, or simply offering a listening ear, these actions reflect a commitment to selflessness and compassion.

Personal Discipline and Self-care

Implementing discipline in daily routines, such as maintaining a spiritual practice, exercising, proper rest, and nourishing the body with healthy food, supports holistic well-being. Prioritizing self-care ensures individuals have the energy and clarity to engage in spiritual pursuits.

Transforming Challenges into Opportunities for Growth

Viewing challenges and difficulties as opportunities for growth and learning aligns with the sanctification process. Embracing adversity with resilience, patience, and faith helps individuals navigate life's ups and downs while maintaining spiritual integrity.

Cultivating Gratitude and Appreciation

Practicing gratitude daily for the blessings and experiences in life fosters a positive mindset. Acknowledging and appreciating the beauty in both simple and profound aspects of life nurtures a sense of contentment and spiritual fulfillment.

Rituals and Reflection

Incorporating brief rituals or moments of reflection throughout the day serves as checkpoints for spiritual connection. Whether it's a morning prayer, a moment of silence before meals, or an evening reflection, these pauses allow for recentering and reconnection with the divine.

Continuous Learning and Growth

Embracing a mindset of continuous learning and growth encourages spiritual evolution. Reading sacred texts, seeking knowledge, and exploring new perspectives contribute to expanding spiritual understanding and consciousness.

Embracing Unity and Diversity

Recognizing the interconnectedness of all beings and embracing diversity fosters a sense of unity. Respecting and celebrating differences while acknowledging the universal aspects of humanity aligns with sanctification.

Sanctification, as a transformative process, exerts a profound influence on various facets of life, including relationships, work, and personal well-being. Let's explore how sanctification impacts these areas:

Relationships

Sanctification profoundly shapes relationships by fostering empathy, compassion, and a deeper understanding of others. It encourages individuals to view others through a lens of respect and kindness, nurturing healthier interactions.

Enhanced Communication: Through sanctification, individuals learn to communicate with empathy and honesty, leading to more meaningful and harmonious relationships. Active listening, patience, and understanding become central tenets in interactions, fostering deeper connections.

Conflict Resolution: Sanctification promotes forgiveness and reconciliation. It enables individuals to approach conflicts with a compassionate mindset, seeking resolutions that honor both parties' dignity and well-being.

Empathy and Compassion: Developing a sanctified outlook cultivates empathy, allowing individuals to relate to others' experiences and emotions more profoundly. This empathy forms the basis of stronger, more supportive relationships.

Work

Sanctification influences how individuals approach their work, infusing it with purpose, integrity, and ethical considerations.

Ethical Decision-Making: Sanctification guides individuals in making ethical decisions aligned with their spiritual values. This ethical framework influences choices in the workplace, leading to decisions that prioritize integrity and moral principles.

Workplace Relationships: Applying sanctification principles at work encourages a more cooperative and supportive environment. Individuals bring a sense of respect, empathy, and collaboration into their interactions, fostering a positive workplace culture.

Service-oriented Approach: Integrating sanctification leads individuals to view their work as a means of service. This mindset shift, regardless of the profession, fosters a deeper sense of fulfillment and purpose in contributing positively to society.

Personal Well-being

Sanctification significantly impacts personal well-being, nurturing a holistic approach to self-care and fulfillment.

Emotional Resilience: Sanctification fosters emotional resilience by encouraging individuals to seek inner peace, even amidst life's challenges.

Practices like mindfulness and prayer promote emotional stability and balance.

Psychological Health: Engaging in sanctification practices such as meditation or prayer contributes to reduced stress and anxiety levels. These practices encourage a sense of calmness and promote mental clarity.

Physical Health: The integration of sanctification often leads to a focus on physical well-being. Individuals practicing sanctification tend to prioritize activities that nourish their bodies, such as exercise, proper nutrition, and adequate rest.

Spiritual Fulfillment: The pursuit of sanctification results in a deeper sense of spiritual fulfillment and purpose, contributing to overall life satisfaction and contentment.

Maintaining sanctification over time

Maintaining sanctification over time involves a consistent and intentional effort to uphold spiritual values and practices in daily life. Here's a detailed exploration of strategies to sustain sanctification throughout life's journey:

Commitment to Spiritual Practices

Consistent Routine: Establishing a daily routine that includes prayer, meditation, or reflection nurtures spiritual connection. Consistency in these practices reinforces the sanctification journey.

Sacred Texts Study: Regularly studying and reflecting upon sacred texts or spiritual teachings provides guidance and inspiration, aiding in staying aligned with spiritual principles.

Community Engagement:Active involvement in a spiritual community offers support, shared learning, and accountability, fostering sustained spiritual growth.

Regular Self-Assessment and Accountability

Introspection: Regular self-reflection aids in assessing personal growth, identifying areas for improvement, and reaffirming commitment to the sanctification path.

Accountability Partnerships: Having mentors, spiritual guides, or accountability partners helps maintain focus and commitment, providing encouragement and support along the journey.

Living Ethically and Compassionately

Upholding Ethical Standards: Consistently applying ethical principles derived from spiritual teachings guides decision-making and behavior, reinforcing sanctification.

Acts of Kindness: Engaging in regular acts of service and compassion towards others cultivates a sense of purpose and reinforces the value of selflessness.

Embracing Change and Growth

Adaptability: Embracing life's changes while staying true to sanctification requires flexibility and adaptability in response to evolving circumstances.

Continuous Learning:Maintaining a thirst for knowledge, seeking new perspectives, and being open to growth contribute to spiritual evolution.

Prioritizing Inner Peace and Resilience

Mindfulness and Presence: Regular mindfulness practices foster inner peace and emotional resilience, aiding in managing stress and challenges.

Holistic Self-Care: Prioritizing self-care in all aspects—physical, emotional, and mental—sustains the capacity for spiritual growth.

Reflective Practice and Gratitude

Periodic Reflection: Periodically reviewing one's spiritual journey, acknowledging progress, and redefining goals supports sustained focus and commitment.

Cultivating Gratitude: Practicing gratitude for the blessings and lessons in life reinforces a positive mindset and the significance of the spiritual path.

Maintaining sanctification requires dedication, consistency, and a steadfast commitment to embodying spiritual values in daily life. It's an ongoing journey that demands continual self-reflection, a supportive community, ethical living, adaptability, and nurturing personal well-being. By integrating these strategies into daily routines, individuals can sustain sanctification and experience continued spiritual growth throughout their lives.

Conclusion

Recap of the transformative journey

Recapping the transformative journey through personal and spiritual growth:

Beginning the Journey:

1. Self-Discovery and Awakening:

   - Discuss the initial phase of the journey marked by self-discovery, curiosity, or a pivotal moment leading to an awakening.

- Explore the impact of this awakening on the individual's perception of life, purpose, or spiritual beliefs.

2. Seeking Guidance and Knowledge:

- Emphasize the role of seeking guidance, mentors, or sources of wisdom that contributed to the individual's growth.

- Discuss the importance of acquiring knowledge and insights that initiated the transformative process.

Challenges and Growth:

1. Facing Obstacles and Doubts:

- Highlight the challenges encountered, such as doubts, setbacks, or internal conflicts, and their role in shaping resilience and determination.

- Discuss how these obstacles became catalysts for introspection and growth.

2. Embracing Change and Adaptability:

- Discuss the transformative impact of embracing change and adapting to new perspectives, experiences, or life circumstances.

- Emphasize the significance of flexibility and openness to new possibilities in the journey.

Integration and Application:

1. Incorporating Spiritual Practices:

  - Explore how spiritual practices like meditation, prayer, or self-reflection became integral parts of the individual's daily routine.

  - Discuss the impact of these practices on nurturing a deeper spiritual connection.

2. Applying Lessons and Values:

  - Highlight how the lessons learned along the journey translated into tangible values and principles applied in daily life.

  - Discuss the significance of living in alignment with newfound beliefs and values.

Transformation and Impact:

1. Personal Growth and Well-being:

  - Emphasize the transformative impact on personal well-being, including emotional resilience, mental clarity, and a sense of purpose.

  - Discuss how the journey contributed to overall happiness and fulfillment.

2. Relationships and Community Impact:

  - Explore how the transformative journey influenced relationships, fostering deeper connections, empathy, and a supportive community.

- Highlight the impact of personal growth on positively influencing those around the individual.

Encouragement and motivation for continued growth

Continued growth in sanctification, although rewarding, often requires encouragement and motivation to stay committed to the spiritual journey. Here's an exploration of ways to sustain enthusiasm and dedication:

Reminders of Progress

Reflection on Growth: Regularly reflecting on one's spiritual journey and acknowledging progress made in embodying spiritual principles serves as a motivational tool. Recognizing personal growth encourages continued commitment.

Celebrating Milestones: Acknowledging and celebrating milestones, no matter how small, reaffirms the significance of the journey and provides encouragement to persist.

Community Support and Encouragement

Community Engagement: Active participation in a supportive spiritual community offers encouragement, guidance, and shared experiences, fostering a sense of belonging and motivation.

Sharing Experiences: Sharing personal experiences and insights within the community not only provides encouragement to others but also reinforces one's commitment to the journey.

nspiration from Spiritual Sources

Sacred Texts and Teachings: Delving deeper into sacred texts or spiritual teachings often serves as a wellspring of inspiration. Extracting wisdom from these sources can reignite enthusiasm and dedication.

Inspirational Figures:Learning about or connecting with individuals who exemplify sanctification can serve as a source of motivation. Their stories and teachings often provide inspiration to continue the journey.

Practicing Gratitude and Mindfulness

Gratitude Practice: Cultivating gratitude for the spiritual journey itself and the blessings encountered along the way reinforces the significance and joy of the sanctification process.

Mindfulness and Present Awareness: Embracing the present moment through mindfulness practices cultivates appreciation for the ongoing growth and encourages perseverance.

Encouragement Through Challenges

Embracing Challenges: Viewing challenges as opportunities for learning and growth encourages perseverance. Overcoming obstacles strengthens resolve and commitment to sanctification.

Learning from Setbacks: Accepting setbacks as part of the journey and learning from them fosters resilience and motivates continued effort towards spiritual growth.

Personal Accountability and Goal Setting

Setting Spiritual Goals:Establishing achievable yet challenging spiritual goals provides direction and motivation for continued growth.

Accountability Practices:Holding oneself accountable through regular self-assessment and reflection helps maintain focus and dedication to the sanctification path.

Embodying Compassion and Service

Acts of Service: Engaging in acts of service and compassion towards others not only aligns with sanctification principles but also generates a sense of fulfillment and motivation to continue.

Empathy and Compassion: Cultivating empathy and compassion towards oneself and others reinforces the importance of the sanctification journey and fosters an environment conducive to growth.

Continuous Learning and Adaptability

Seeking New Perspectives:Embracing a mindset of continuous learning and seeking diverse perspectives keeps the journey dynamic and encourages ongoing growth.

Adaptability: Being open to new experiences and adapting to changes on the spiritual path supports sustained motivation and growth.

Encouragement and motivation for continued growth in sanctification stem from various sources—personal reflections, community support, spiritual teachings, gratitude practices, embracing challenges, setting goals, and embodying compassion. By integrating these elements into the sanctification journey, individuals can find renewed enthusiasm, dedication, and motivation to persist and flourish in their spiritual development.

Final thoughts and encouragement for readers

Absolutely, embarking on the journey of sanctification is a profound commitment towards personal growth, spiritual enrichment, and embodying higher principles. As we conclude this exploration, here are some final thoughts and words of encouragement:

Embracing the Journey

The path of sanctification is not a destination but a continuous journey, a lifelong pursuit of spiritual growth and transformation. It's a journey that demands patience, resilience, and unwavering commitment. Embrace each step, regardless of its size, for every moment contributes to the evolution of the soul.

Embracing Imperfection

Remember, sanctification isn't about achieving perfection but about striving towards spiritual growth amidst our imperfections. Embrace your humanity, acknowledging that setbacks and challenges are an integral part of the journey. It's through these moments that we learn, grow, and deepen our understanding of ourselves and the divine.

Cultivating Compassion and Empathy

At the heart of sanctification lies the cultivation of compassion and empathy—towards oneself and others. Practice kindness, forgiveness, and understanding. Extend compassion not only to those around you but also towards yourself as you navigate the complexities of life's journey.

Finding Strength in Community

Seek support and strength in your spiritual community. Engage with like-minded individuals who share the same pursuit of spiritual growth. Together, you can inspire, learn, and support each other through shared experiences and wisdom.

Embracing Change and Adaptability

Be open to change and embrace the lessons it brings. Adaptability fosters growth and resilience. Challenges are opportunities for growth; they shape us into more compassionate, understanding, and stronger individuals.

Gratitude for the Journey

Cultivate gratitude for every experience, every lesson, and every moment on this journey. Gratitude fuels a positive mindset and reinforces the significance of the sanctification process.

Continual Learning and Reflection

Stay curious and embrace the opportunity for continual learning. Reflect on your experiences, celebrate your growth, and reassess your goals. Let self-reflection guide you on this profound journey of spiritual evolution.

Trusting the Process

Lastly, trust the process. There might be moments of doubt or uncertainty, but trust that each step taken in the direction of sanctification is shaping you into the person you aspire to be.

In essence, the pursuit of sanctification is a deeply personal and transformative journey—one that requires dedication, courage, and an unwavering commitment to spiritual growth. As you continue along this path, may you find fulfillment, peace, and a deeper connection with the divine. Embrace the journey wholeheartedly, knowing that every step taken is a step towards greater spiritual fulfillment and alignment with the sacred.

www.ingramcontent.com/pod-product-compliance
Lightning Source LLC
Chambersburg PA
CBHW062253290526
45794CB00006B/2537